Music Theory Practice Paper 2022 Grade 4
Model Answers

1 Rhythm

1.1 (a) **12/8** (3)

(b) **3/8**

(c) **𝄵**

1.2 (1)

1.3 (a) 3 (2)

(b) 1

1.4 (1)

1.5 (3)

2 Pitch

/10

2.1 (a) D double flat

(4)

(b) F double sharp

(c) B sharp

(d) A natural

2.2

(2)

2.3 (a) **FALSE**

(2)

(b) **FALSE**

2.4

(2)

(a)

(b)

3 Keys and Scales

/15

3.1

(1)

3.2

(1)

Grade

4

ABRSM

Music Theory Practice Papers 2022

Model Answers

ABRSM Grade 4

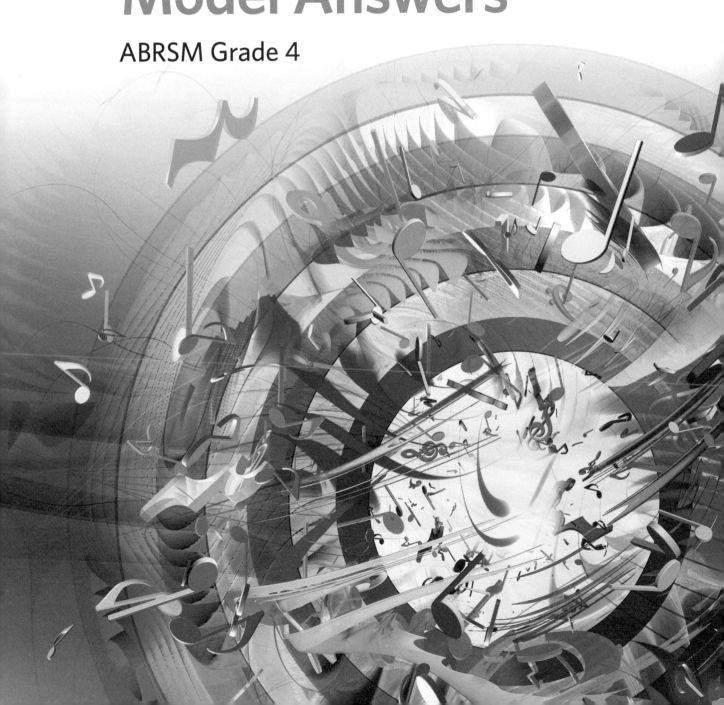

Music Theory Practice Papers Model Answers

These model answer papers have been created to work alongside our Music Theory Practice Papers 2022 to help prepare candidates for our online Music Theory exams.

For general advice on taking theory exams, please refer to www.abrsm.org/theory.

Using these answers

- Answers are given in the same order and, where possible, in the same layout as in the exam papers, making it easy to match answer to question.

- For added clarity, in multiple-choice answers where the answers are similar, all options are shown in grey with the answer presented in black, for example:

© 2022 by The Associated Board of the Royal Schools of Music
Published by ABRSM (Publishing) Ltd, a wholly owned subsidiary of ABRSM
Cover by Andy Potts
Music and text setting by Pete Readman
Printed in England by Caligraving Ltd, Thetford, Norfolk, on materials from sustainable sources
P15772

3.3 (a) F minor   (3)

  (b) D♭ major

  (c) C♯ minor

3.4 (a) **FALSE**   (2)

  (b) **FALSE**

3.5 X G♯   (2)

  Y A♯

3.6   (2)

(a)

(b)

3.7 (a) FALSE

(4)

    (b) **TRUE**

    (c) **TRUE**

    (d) **FALSE**

4 Intervals

/10

4.1

(6)

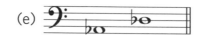

4.2 (a) minor

(4)

    (b) diminished

    (c) perfect

    (d) major

5 Triads/Chords

/10

5.1 (a) TRUE

(4)

    (b) **FALSE**

    (c) **FALSE**

    (d) **TRUE**

5.2 (a) IV   (b) V   (c) IV   (3)

5.3   ⬚ I   ⬚ IV   ⬚ I   (3)

6 Terms, Signs and Instruments   /10

6.1   (3)

come prima means:	**risoluto** means:	**tempo comodo** means:
as before	bold, strong	at a comfortable speed

6.2 animato   (1)

6.3 acciaccatura   (1)

6.4 (a) **TRUE**   (5)

     (b) **FALSE**

     (c) **TRUE**

     (d) **FALSE**

     (e) **FALSE**

7 Music in Context   /10

7.1 (a) 5   (5)

     (b) 4

     (c) 3

     (d) 3

     (e) 1

7.2 (a) **FALSE**   (3)

     (b) **FALSE**

     (c) **TRUE**

7.3

(1)

 ✔

7.4

(1)

 ✔

Music Theory Practice Paper 2022 Grade 4 B
Model Answers

1 Rhythm   /10

1.1 (a) $\dfrac{3}{2}$ (3)

   (b) $\dfrac{9}{8}$

   (c) $\dfrac{6}{16}$

1.2   (1)

1.3 (a) 7   (2)

   (b) 4

1.4   (1)

1.5   (3)

2 Pitch

2.1 (a) G flat   (4)

    (b) C sharp

    (c) G double flat

    (d) E natural

2.2   (2)

2.3 (a) **TRUE**   (2)

    (b) **FALSE**

2.4   (2)

3 Keys and Scales

3.1   (1)

3.2   (1)

3.3 (a) E major $\hspace{4cm}$ (3)

(b) B♭ minor

(c) G minor

3.4 (a) **TRUE** $\hspace{4cm}$ (2)

(b) **FALSE**

3.5 X A♭ $\hspace{4cm}$ (2)

$\hspace{0.5cm}$ **Y** E

3.6 $\hspace{8cm}$ (2)

(a)

(b)

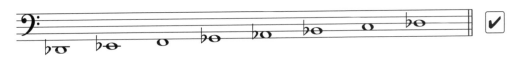

3.7 (a) **FALSE** (4)

(b) **FALSE**

(c) **TRUE**

(d) **TRUE**

4 Intervals /10

4.1 (6)

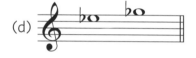 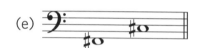 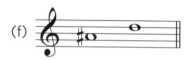

4.2 (a) perfect (4)

(b) augmented

(c) major

(d) major

5 Triads/Chords /10

5.1 (a) **FALSE** (4)

(b) **TRUE**

(c) **TRUE**

(d) **FALSE**

5.2 (a) IV   (b) V   (c) I   (3)

5.3 | I | | IV | | V | (3)

6 Terms, Signs and Instruments   /10

6.1   (3)

stringendo means: **con brio** means: **semplice** means:

gradually getting faster   with vigour, lively   simple, plain

6.2 moderato   (1)

6.3 grace notes   (1)

6.4 (a) **TRUE**   (5)

(b) **FALSE**

(c) **FALSE**

(d) **TRUE**

(e) **FALSE**

7 Music in Context   /10

7.1 (a) 6   (5)

(b) 4

(c) 7

(d) 5

(e) 1

7.2 (a) **TRUE**   (3)

(b) **FALSE**

(c) **FALSE**

7.3

(1)

7.4

(1)

Music Theory Practice Paper 2022 Grade 4 C
Model Answers

1 Rhythm /10

1.1 (a) **6/8** (3)

(b) **12/8**

(c) **2/4**

1.2 (1)

1.3 (a) 7 (2)

(b) 2

1.4 (1)

1.5 (3)

2 Pitch

2.1 (a) A sharp

(4)

(b) D double flat

(c) B double sharp

(d) E natural

2.2

(2)

2.3 (a) **TRUE**

(2)

(b) **TRUE**

2.4

(2)

(a)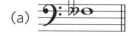

(b)

3 Keys and Scales

3.1

(1)

3.2

(1)

3.3 (a) F♯ minor   (3)

(b) F minor

(c) E major

3.4 (a) **TRUE**   (2)

(b) **FALSE**

3.5 X E♯   (2)

   Y F𝄪

3.6   (2)

(a)

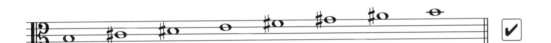

(b)

3.7 (a) **TRUE**

(b) **FALSE**

(c) **TRUE**

(d) **FALSE**

(4)

4 Intervals

/10

4.1

(6)

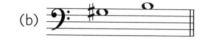

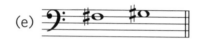

4.2 (a) diminished

(b) augmented

(c) perfect

(d) perfect

(4)

5 Triads/Chords

/10

5.1 (a) **TRUE**

(b) **FALSE**

(c) **TRUE**

(d) **FALSE**

(4)

5.2 (a) V   (b) I   (c) IV   (3)

5.3   V   I   IV   (3)

6 Terms, Signs and Instruments   /10

6.1   (3)

retenu means: *leggiero* means: **più mosso** means:

held back   light   more movement, quicker

6.2 triste   (1)

6.3 upper turn   (1)

6.4 (a) **TRUE**   (5)

(b) **FALSE**

(c) **TRUE**

(d) **TRUE**

(e) **TRUE**

7 Music in Context   /10

7.1 (a) 2   (5)

(b) 80

(c) 6

(d) 6

(e) 7

7.2 (a) **FALSE**   (3)

(b) **TRUE**

(c) **FALSE**

7.3

7.4

Music Theory Practice Paper 2022 Grade 4 D
Model Answers

1 Rhythm /10

1.1 (a) $\frac{3}{4}$ (3)

(b) $\frac{3}{8}$

(c) $\frac{9}{4}$

1.2 (1)

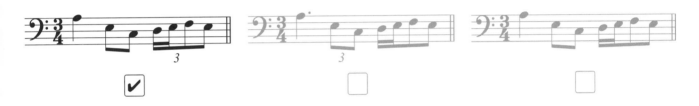

1.3 (a) 2 (2)

(b) 2

1.4 (1)

1.5 (3)

2 Pitch

2.1 (a) D double sharp   (4)

(b) G flat

(c) A sharp

(d) E natural

2.2   (2)

2.3 (a) **TRUE**   (2)

(b) **TRUE**

2.4   (2)

3 Keys and Scales

/15

3.1   (1)

3.2   (1)

3.3 (a) B major   (3)

    (b) E minor

    (c) F minor

3.4 (a) **FALSE**   (2)

    (b) **FALSE**

3.5 X E   (2)

  Y F×

3.6   (2)

(a)

(b)

3.7 (a) **TRUE** (4)

(b) **TRUE**

(c) **FALSE**

(d) **FALSE**

4 Intervals

/10

4.1 (6)

(a)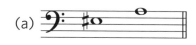

(b)

(c)

(d)

(e)

(f)

4.2 (a) minor (4)

(b) augmented

(c) perfect

(d) minor

5 Triads/Chords

/10

5.1 (a) **FALSE** (4)

(b) **TRUE**

(c) **FALSE**

(d) **FALSE**

5.2 (a) IV (b) IV (c) V (3)

5.3 | I | | IV | | V | (3)

6 Terms, Signs and Instruments /10

6.1 (3)

allargando means:

broadening

tristamente means:

sad, sorrowful

amabile means:

pleasant

6.2 *douce* (1)

6.3 upper mordent (1)

6.4 (a) **FALSE** (5)

(b) **TRUE**

(c) **FALSE**

(d) **FALSE**

(e) **FALSE**

7 Music in Context /10

7.1 (a) 14 (5)

(b) 3

(c) 6

(d) 7

(e) 7

7.2 (a) **TRUE** (3)

(b) **TRUE**

(c) **FALSE**

7.3

7.4

Music Theory Practice Papers 2022 Model Answers

Model answers for practice papers for ABRSM's Grade 4 Theory exams

Support material for ABRSM Music Theory exams

- Music Theory Practice Papers 2022
- Music Theory Practice Papers 2021
- Music Theory Practice Papers 2021 Model Answers
- Music Theory Sample Papers
- Music Theory Sample Papers Model Answers
- More Music Theory Sample Papers
- More Music Theory Sample Papers Model Answers

Visit the website for everything you need to prepare for your next Music Theory exam.

Supporting the teaching and learning of music
in partnership with four Royal Schools of Music

Royal Academy of Music | Royal College of Music
Royal Northern College of Music | Royal Conservatoire of Scotland

www.abrsm.org f facebook.com/abrsm
🐦 @abrsm ▶ ABRSM YouTube

ISBN 978-1-78601-541-9

9 781786 015419